Rod Ste~ Quiz Bo~~

101 Questions To Test Your Knowledge Of This Incredibly Successful Musician

By Colin Carter

Rod Stewart Quiz

This book contains one hundred and fifty informative and entertaining trivia questions with multiple choice answers. With 150 questions, some easy, some more demanding, this entertaining book will really test your knowledge of Rod Stewart.

You will be quizzed on a wide range of topics associated with Rod for you to test yourself; with questions on his early days, his songs, his lyrics, his achievements, his awards and much more, guaranteeing you a truly fun, educational experience.

This quiz book will provide entertainment for fans of all ages and will certainly test your knowledge of this world-famous musician. The book is packed with information and is a must-have for all true Rod Stewart fans, wherever you live in the world.

Published by Glowworm Press
glowwormpress.com

FOREWORD

When I was asked to write a foreword to this book, I was incredibly flattered.

I have known Colin for several years and his knowledge of facts and figures is phenomenal.

His love for music and his talent for writing quiz books makes him the ideal man to pay homage to the genius that is Sir Rod Stewart.

This book came about because of a challenge during a round of golf!

I do hope you enjoy the book.

Jon Stradders

Here is the first set of questions.

Q1. Where was Rod Stewart born?
A) Dublin
B) Glasgow
C) Edinburgh
D) London

Q2. When was Rod Stewart born?
A) 1941
B) 1943
C) 1945
D) 1947

Q3. What is Rod Stewart's full name?
A) Robert Douglas Stewart
B) Roderick David Stewart
C) Rodney James Stewart
D) Ronald Daniel Stewart

Q4. How many records has Rod Stewart sold
worldwide?
A) 90 million
B) 100 million
C) 110 million
D) 120 million

Q5. How many UK number one albums has Rod Stewart had?

A) 4

B) 6

C) 8

D) 10

Q6. How many UK number one singles has Rod Stewart had?

A) 4

B) 6

C) 8

D) 10

Q7. How many US number one albums has Rod Stewart had?

A) 1

B) 2

C) 3

D) 4

Q8. How many US number one singles has Rod Stewart had?

A) 2

B) 4

C) 6

D) 8

Q9. What was the first musical instruments Rod learnt to play?
A) Guitar
B) Harmonica
C) Piano
D) Violin

Q10. What was the name of Rod Stewart's first band?
A) Steampacket
B) The Dimensions
C) The Hoochie Coochie Men
D) The Raiders

Here is the first set of answers and if you get seven or more right, you are doing well.

A1. Rod Stewart was born in Highgate, London, England. Growing up in the capital provided him with exposure to a diverse range of musical influences and opportunities, ultimately shaping his artistic development and contributing to his eventual success in the global music industry.

A2. Rod was born on 10th January 1945.

A3. Rod Stewart's full name is Roderick David Stewart, reflecting his Scottish and English heritage.

A4. According to Wikipedia, Rod has sold over 120 million records.

A5. Rod has had 10 UK number one albums, showcasing his enduring popularity.

A6. Rod has had 6 UK number one singles, including 31 top-ten singles.

A7. Rod has had 3 US number one albums in the Billboard charts.

A8. Rod has had 4 US number one singles, including 16 top-ten singles.

A9. Rod learned to play the harmonica when he was a youngster. Learning to play an instrument played a pivotal role in shaping his musical sensibilities and development as an artist.

A10. Although Wikipedia lists Rod's first band as The Dimensions, the real story is quite different. Rod clarified a lot of his early days in his autobiography. Initially Rod appeared briefly with The Raiders, Jimmy Powell & The Five Dimensions, then in 1964 made his first known recording with The Hoochie Coochie Men (Long John Baldry's band). This band then evolved into Steampacket, before Rod moved to Shotgun Express joining Beryl Marsden and pre-Fleetwood Mac musicians Mick Fleetwood and Peter Greene. He was then in The Soul Agents for a short while, and then Peter B's Looners. Give yourself a point for any answer!

Here is the next set of questions.

Q11. What year did Rod join The Jeff Beck Group?
A) 1964
B) 1965
C) 1966
D) 1967

Q12. Which band did Rod join after leaving the Jeff Beck Group?
A) Ears
B) Faces
B) Legs
D) Noses

Q13. Which of these songs is Rod credited (along with Ronnie Wood) with writing?
A) Cindy Incidentally
B) (I Know) I'm Losing You
C) Ooh La La
D) Stay with Me

Q14. What is the name of Rod's first solo album?
A) An Old Raincoat Won't Ever Let You Down
B) Every Picture Tells a Story
C) Gasoline Alley
D) Never a Dull Moment

Q15. What is the name of Rod's second solo album?
A) A Night On The Town
B) Every Picture Tells a Story
C) Gasoline Alley
D) Smiler

Q16. What is the name of Rod's third solo album?
A) A Night On The Town
B) Atlantic Crossing
C) Every Picture Tells a Story
D) Never a Dull Moment

Q17. Which album is a sequel to "Every Picture Tells a Story"?
A) A Night on the Town
B) Footloose & Fancy Free
C) Never a Dull Moment
D) Smiler

Q18. When did Rod first reach the top of the UK singles chart?
A) 1969
B) 1971
C) 1975
D) 1979

Q19. Which album features the hit "You Wear It Well"?
A) Every Picture Tells a Story
B) Gasoline Alley
C) Never a Dull Moment
D) Smiler

Q20. What was the name of Rod's 1977 album?
A) Body Wishes
B) Foot Loose & Fancy Free
C) Never a Dull Moment
D) Smiler

Here is the latest set of answers.

A11. The original 1967 line-up of the The Jeff Beck Group included Rod Stewart as the vocalist, bassist Ronnie Wood, and lead guitarist Jeff Beck. Drummers changed often but their longest standing drummer was Micky Waller. Jeff Beck is best known for his hit "Hi-Ho Silver Lining" where Rod provided backing vocals.

A12. Before embarking on a successful solo career, Rod Stewart was a member of the influential rock band Faces. The band, known for their energetic live performances and raw, blues-infused sound, played a significant role in shaping rock music in the early 1970s. Faces were formed in 1969 by members of Small Faces after their lead singer and guitarist Steve Marriott left to form Humble Pie. The remaining Small Faces - Ian McLagan on keyboard, Ronnie Lane on bass guitar, and drummer Kenney Jones were joined by lead guitarist Ronnie Wood and singer Rod Stewart, both from The Jeff Beck Group, and the new line-up was renamed Faces.

A13. Rod Stewart and Ronnie Wood are credited with co-writing "Stay with Me" for Faces, which became one of their signature hits.

A14. Rod's first solo album titled "An Old Raincoat Won't Ever Let You Down," was released in 1969. This album marked the beginning of his successful solo career, showcasing his distinctive voice and stylistic range, and laying the groundwork for his future musical work.

A15. Rod's second solo album is titled "Gasoline Alley". It was released in 1970. It is a mix of covers and compositions by Rod. It featured significant musical contributions from the other members of his band Faces.

A16. Rod's third solo album was titled "Every Picture Tells a Story". It was released in 1971 and it incorporates hard rock, folk, and blues styles. It features the hit single "Maggie May."

A17. "Never a Dull Moment", Rod's fourth album, is considered a sequel to "Every Picture Tells a Story," as it maintains a similar musical style.

A18. Rod first topped the UK singles chart in 1971 with "Maggie May." This song is one of his signature tunes and remains popular, illustrating his enduring appeal and the timeless nature of his music.

A19. "You Wear It Well" is a hit song from Rod's fourth solo album "Never a Dull Moment" which was released in 1972.

A20. "Foot Loose & Fancy Free" was released in 1977, featuring hits like "You're In My Heart."

Here is the next set of questions.

Q21. Which album does "The Killing of Georgie" appear on?
A) A Night on the Town
B) Atlantic Crossing
C) Every Picture Tells a Story
D) Foot Loose & Fancy Free

Q22. Which album did Rod release in 1975 that marked a departure from his established rock sound?
A) A Night on the Town
B) Atlantic Crossing
C) Body Wishes
D) Foot Loose & Fancy Free

Q23. Who originally recorded "I Don't Want to Talk About It"?
A) Crazy Horse
B) Fleetwood Mac
C) Lynyrd Skynyrd
D) The Eagles

Q24. When was the album "Blondes Have More Fun" released?
A) 1972

B) 1974
C) 1976
D) 1978

Q25. Who was the producer of the "Blondes Have More Fun" album?
A) Tom Dowd
B) Trevor Horn
C) George Martin
D) Mickie Most

Q26. Who is credited with playing the slide guitar on "Maggie May"?
A) Jeff Beck
B) Ray Jackson
C) Martin Quittenton
D) Ronnie Wood

Q27. Which was Rod's first number one album in the UK?
A) An Old Raincoat Won't Ever Let You Down
B) Every Picture Tells a Story
C) Gasoline Alley
D) Never a Dull Moment

Q28. What was Rod's first number one album in the US?

A) A Night on the Town
B) Blondes Have More Fun
C) Every Picture Tells a Story
D) Gasoline Alley

Q29. What was Rod's first number one single in the USA?
A) Da Ya Think I'm Sexy?
B) Maggie May
C) Tonight's the Night
D) You're In My Heart

Q30. Who originally wrote "The First Cut Is the Deepest"?
A) P.P. Arnold
B) Sheryl Crow
C) Bob Dylan
D) Cat Stevens

Here is the latest set of answers.

A21. "The Killing of Georgie" is a track from the album "A Night on the Town," which was released in 1976.

A22. "Atlantic Crossing" marked a departure from Rod Stewart's established rock sound as he explored a more polished, radio-friendly and disco-infused sound. This album, released in 1975, represents Rod's movement towards a more mainstream audience, combining elements of rock, pop, and soul music.

A23. "I Don't Want to Talk About It" was originally recorded by American rock band Crazy Horse in 1971. Rod's version, which featured on the Atlantic Crossing album, became a huge hit a few years later.

A24. "Blondes Have More Fun" was released in 1978. This album exemplifies Rod's exploration of disco influences and his ability to traverse different musical genres, reflecting the evolving musical landscape of the time.

A25 The legendary producer Tom Dowd was at the helm for Rod's "Blondes Have More Fun" album.

A26. Ronnie Wood is credited with playing the slide guitar on "Maggie May."

A27. Rod achieved his first UK number one album with "Every Picture Tells a Story" released in 1971. This album's commercial success marked a significant milestone in his career, solidifying his status as a leading musical artist and showcasing his storytelling abilities and musical versatility.

A28 "Every Picture Tells a Story" also achieved the number one position on the US chart in 1971, becoming his first album to do so.

A29. "Maggie May" achieved the number one spot in the USA, marking Rod's first chart-topping hit in the country.

A30. "The First Cut Is the Deepest" was written by Cat Stevens in 1967. Rod's version was released in 1977 and it went on to be a huge hit.

Let's have some questions about Rod's personal life.

Q31. What was Rod's first job before he became a musician?
A) A bartender
B) A gravedigger
C) A newspaper delivery boy
D) A tailor

Q32. How many times has Rod been married?
A) Three
B) Four
C) Five
D) Six

Q33. How many children does Rod have?
A) 5
B) 6
C) 7
D) 8

Q34. What is the name of Rod's first wife?
A) Britt Ekland
B) Dee Harrington
C) Rachel Hunter
C) Alana Stewart

Q35. What is the name of Rod's eldest daughter?
A) Kimberly
B) Renee
C) Ruby
D) Sarah

Q36. Which football club does Rod support?
A) Celtic
B) Charlton
C) Chelsea
D) Crystal Palace

Q37. Who is the mother of Rod's first child, Sarah Streeter?
A) Susannah Boffey
B) Britt Ekland
C) Rachel Hunter
D) Alana Stewart

Q38. What is the name of Rod's second wife?
A) Britt Ekland
B) Kelly Emberg
C) Rachel Hunter
D) Jennie Rylance

Q39. What is the name of Rod's third wife?

A) Penny Baker
C) Penny Lane
C) Penny Lancaster
D) Penny Taylor

Q40. What kind of model-building does Rod enjoy as a hobby?
A) Model airplanes
B) Model cars
C) Model ships
D) Model trains

Here are the answers to the last set of questions.

A31. Before embarking on his illustrious music career, Rod did several jobs including working in the family shop and as a newspaper delivery boy. He then worked briefly as a labourer for Highgate Cemetery, which became part of his biographical lore as it was reported he was a gravedigger, which Rod later stated was not the case.

A32. Rod has been married three times. His marriages have been well-publicised, reflecting the intersections between his personal life and public persona as a major music icon.

A33. Rod has a large family with a total of eight children from various relationships.

A34. Rod's first wife is called Alana Stewart. They were married from 1979 to 1984.

A35. Sarah Streeter is the name of Rod's eldest daughter. Sarah was adopted shortly after birth, and their relationship has been the subject of public interest and discussion, reflecting the intersections of personal narratives and public life of a celebrity.

A36. Rod is a renowned fan of Celtic Football Club. His passion for the team is well-known, and he has been spotted at numerous games.

A37. Susannah Boffey is the mother of Rod's oldest child, Sarah Streeter. Sarah was born when both her parents were very young, and she was initially placed up for adoption, but in later years, she reconnected with her biological parents.

A38. Rod's second wife was former New Zealand super model Rachel Hunter. They were married from 1990 to 2006. These days, amongst other things, she teaches yoga.

A39. Rod's third wife is Penny Lancaster, whom he married in 2007. The couple wed in a cloistered medieval abbey at La Cervara, just outside Portofino on the Italian Riviera.

A40. Rod is an avid enthusiast of model trains and has created many extensive and detailed model train layouts.

Let's move onto the next set of questions.

Q41. What is Rod's vocal range classified as?
A) Baritone
B) Bass
C) Soprano
D) Tenor

Q42. What is Rod's old nickname?
A) Rod The Clod
B) Rod The Mod
C) Rod The Plod
D) Rod The Sod

Q43. How tall is Rod?
A) 5 feet 4 inches
B) 5 feet 6 inches
C) 5 feet 8 inches
D) 5 feet 10 inches

Q44. Which album includes the hit single "This Old Heart of Mine"?
A) A Night on the Town
B) Atlantic Crossing
C) Blondes Have More Fun
D) Foot Loose & Fancy Free

Q45. Which album features a cover photograph by renowned photographer Annie Leibovitz?
A) A Night on the Town
B) Atlantic Crossing
C) Blondes Have More Fun
D) Foot Loose & Fancy Free

Q46. Which single was released in 1978 and became a huge disco hit?
A) Da Ya Think I'm Sexy?
B) Hot Legs
C) Passion
D) Young Turks

Q47. Who directed the music video for "Da Ya Think I'm Sexy?"?
A) Steve Barron
B) Bruce Gowers
C) Mike Mansfield
D) Russell Mulcahy

Q48. Which album includes the song "Da Ya Think I'm Sexy?"?
A) A Night on the Town
B) Blondes Have More Fun
C) Foolish Behaviour
D) Foot Loose & Fancy Free

Q49. Which of the following songs is included in Rod's album "A Night on the Town"?
A) I'm Losing You
B) Tonight's the Night
C) You're in My Heart
D) Young Turks

Q50. Which year did Rod release "I Don't Want to Talk About It"?
A) 1975
B) 1977
C) 1979
D) 1981

Here is the latest set of answers.

A41. Rod's distinctive raspy voice is classified as a tenor, allowing him to reach high notes with ease.

A42. The nickname 'Rod the Mod' comes from Rod's early association with the 1960s mod subculture.

A43. Rod is 5 feet 10 inches tall, or if you prefer in metric 1.78 metres tall.

A44. The 1975 album "Atlantic Crossing" features the hit single "This Old Heart of Mine."

A45. The album cover for "A Night on the Town" was photographed by Annie Leibovitz.

A46. The single "Da Ya Think I'm Sexy?" was released by Rod in 1978 and quickly became a disco hit. This track, with its catchy chorus and danceable rhythm, represented a departure from his earlier rock sound, reflecting the disco craze of the late 1970s.

A47. The music video for "Da Ya Think I'm Sexy?" was directed by the innovative Bruce Gowers.

A48. "Blondes Have More Fun" includes "Da Ya Think I'm Sexy?" This song, with its infectious melody is one of Rod's most recognised songs, reflecting the diverse range of his musical repertoire.

A49. "Tonight's the Night" is included in the 1976 album "A Night on the Town" and it went on to became one of Rod's biggest hits.

A50. Rod released "I Don't Want to Talk About It" in 1977, adding another emotional and heartfelt song to his repertoire. This song, characterised by its emotive lyrics and melodic composition, highlights Rod's ability to convey deep emotion and create memorable musical experiences, contributing to his lasting appeal as an artist.

Right, here goes with the next set of questions.

Q51. Which album includes the hit single "I Don't Want to Talk About It"?
A) Atlantic Crossing
B) Blondes Have More Fun
C) Foot Loose & Fancy Free
D) Night on the Town

Q52. Which charity did Rod donate his profits from "Da Ya Think I'm Sexy?" to?
A) NSPCC
B) OXFAM
C) UNESCO
D) UNICEF

Q53. Which album features the hit song "Baby Jane"?
A) Body Wishes
B) Camouflage
C) Every Beat of My Heart
D) Out of Order

Q54. Which year did Rod release "Some Guys Have All the Luck"?
A) 1980
B) 1982

C) 1984
D) 1986

Q55. Which of the following songs did Rod Stewart and Jeff Beck collaborate on in 1985?
A) Every Beat of My Heart
B) Infatuation
C) People Get Ready
D) Some Guys Have All the Luck

Q56. Which of Rod's albums was released in 1988?
A) Camouflage
B) Every Beat of My Heart
C) Out of Order
D) Vagabond Heart

Q57. What was Rod's highest charting single of the 1980s?
A) Baby Jane
B) Infatuation
C) Passion
D) Young Turks

Q58. Which of Rod's songs was written for the film 'Legal Eagles'?
A) Infatuation

B) Love Touch
C) Some Guys Have All the Luck
D) Young Turks

Q59. Who did Rod collaborate with on the song "It Takes Two"?
A) Whitney Houston
B) Lisa Stansfield
C) Donna Summer
D) Tina Turner

Q60. When was the album "Vagabond Heart" released?
A) 1991
B) 1993
C) 1995
D) 1997

Here is the latest set of answers.

A51. Rod covered "I Don't Want to Talk About It" on the 1976 "A Night on the Town" album. This song, originally by Crazy Horse, was given a poignant and emotive rendition by Stewart, reflecting his ability to bring depth and vulnerability to his performances.

A52. Royalties from "Da Ya Think I'm Sexy?" were donated to the United Nations Children's Fund (UNICEF).

A53. "Baby Jane" is a hit song from Rod's 1983 album "Body Wishes."

A54. Rod released "Some Guys Have All the Luck" in 1984, adding another hit to his extensive catalog.

A55. Rod Stewart and Jeff Beck collaborated on the song "People Get Ready" in 1985. This song is a cover of the Curtis Mayfield classic, and the collaboration highlighted the synergistic musical chemistry between Stewart and Beck, resonating well with fans of both artists.

A56. "Out of Order" was released in 1988.

A57. "Baby Jane" was Rod's highest-charting song of the 1980s, reaching the top of the charts in several countries.

A58. "Love Touch" was written for the film 'Legal Eagles.' The 1986 film starred Robert Redford, Daryl Hannan and Debra Winger.

A59. Rod performed a duet with Tina Turner for the song "It Takes Two" in 1990. This collaboration combines the explosive energy and distinctive voices of both artists, creating a memorable and dynamic musical experience.

A60. "Vagabond Heart" was released in 1991.

Here is the next set of questions.

Q61. Who inducted Rod Stewart into the US Rock and Roll Hall of Fame in 1994?
A) Jeff Beck
B) Mick Jagger
C) Elton John
D) Paul McCartney

Q62. Who did Rod collaborate with for the song "All for Love"?
A) Bryan Adams and Sting
B) David Bowie and Mick Jagger
C) Eric Clapton and Paul McCartney
D) Phil Collins and Elton John

Q63. When did Rod receive his star on the Hollywood Walk of Fame?
A) 2003
B) 2005
C) 2007
D) 2009

Q64. Which music award did Rod receive in 2005?
A) American Music Award
B) BRIT Award for Outstanding Contribution to Music

C) Grammy Award
D) MTV Video Music Award

Q65. Which song did Rod perform at the opening of the 2014 Commonwealth Games?
A) Forever Young
B) Maggie May
C) Rhythm of My Heart
D) Sailing

Q66. What genre is Rod's album "Another Country" primarily?
A) Country
B) Folk
C) Pop
D) Rock

Q67. Which of Rod's songs has a music video set in a circus?
A) Baby Jane
B) Some Guys Have All the Luck
C) Tonight I'm Yours
D) Young Turks

Q68. Which Las Vegas hotel has Rod had a residency in?
A) Aria

B) Caesars Palace
C) Mandalay Bay
D) The Venetian

Q69. Who was Rod's musical idol growing up?
A) Sam Cooke
B) Buddy Holly
C) Elvis Presley
D) Little Richard

Q70. Which year was the album "A Spanner in the Works" released?
A) 1993
B) 1995
C) 1997
D) 1999

Here is the latest set of answers.

A61. Rod was inducted into the Rock and Roll Hall of Fame in 1994 by Jeff Beck. Rod was also inducted into the UK Music Hall of Fame in 2006 and inducted a second time into the US Rock and Roll Hall of Fame in 2012 as a member of Faces.

A62. Rod collaborated with Bryan Adams and Sting for the song "All for Love" as the soundtrack for the 1993 movie 'The Three Musketeers' starring Charlie Sheen, Chris O'Donnell and Kiefer Sutherland amongst others.

A63. Rod was honoured with a star on the Hollywood Walk of Fame in 2005. This acknowledgment commemorated his contributions to the music industry and his enduring impact on popular culture.

A64. Rod was honoured with the BRIT Award for Outstanding Contribution to Music in 2005.

A65. Rod performed "Rhythm of My Heart" at the opening ceremony of the 2014 Commonwealth Games, adding his unique flair to the event. The song's upbeat and heartfelt melody resonated with the themes of unity and camaraderie inherent in the games.

A66. "Another Country," released in 2015, is primarily a rock album, though it does blend various musical influences.

A67. The music video for "Baby Jane" is set in a vibrant circus, showcasing an array of characters and performances.

A68. Rod Stewart had two successful residencies at Caesars Palace in Las Vegas, showcasing his greatest hits. The residency, known as 'Rod Stewart: The Hits.' showcased Rod's extensive and diverse catalog of iconic hits, providing fans with a unique and intimate experience in one of the entertainment capitals of the world.

A69. Growing up, Rod idolised Elvis Presley and was heavily influenced by his music and style.

A70. Rod released the album "A Spanner in the Works" in 1995, experimenting with different musical styles.

Here is the next block of questions.

Q71. How many Great American Songbook albums has Rod recorded?
A) 2
B) 3
C) 4
D) 5

Q72. Who dueted with Rod for a version of "Bewitched, Bothered and Bewildered"?
A) Paula Abdul
B) Cher
C) Cyndi Lauper
D) Kylie Minogue

Q73. Who dueted with Rod for a version of "I've Got A Crush On You"?
A) Chaka Khan
B) Kylie Minogue
C) Diana Ross
D) Donna Summer

Q74. Which album includes a duet with Dolly Parton on the song "Baby, It's Cold Outside"?
A) It Had to Be You: The Great American Songbook

B) As Time Goes By: The Great American
Songbook, Volume II
C) Stardust: The Great American Songbook,
Volume III
D) Thanks for the Memory: The Great American
Songbook, Volume IV

Q75. Which album includes a version of "Blue
Moon"?
A) It Had to Be You: The Great American
Songbook
B) As Time Goes By: The Great American
Songbook, Volume II
C) Stardust: The Great American Songbook,
Volume III
D) Fly Me to the Moon: The Great American
Songbook Volume V

Q76. Which album includes the song "You Wear It
Well"?
A) Atlantic Crossing
B) Gasoline Alley
C) Never a Dull Moment
D) Smiler

Q77. Which song on the "Never A Dull Moment"
album discusses the life of a mod in the 1960s?

A) French Girls
B) German Girls
C) Italian Girls
D) Spanish Girls

Q78. Which of Rod's albums includes the hit "Rhythm of My Heart"?
A) A Spanner in the Works
B) Out of Order
C) Vagabond Heart
D) When We Were the New Boys

Q79. Which of Rod's albums includes a cover of the song "Purple Heather"?
A) An Old Raincoat Won't Ever Let You Down
B) Gasoline Alley
C) Every Picture Tells a Story
D) Never a Dull Moment

Q80. What was the lead single from Rod's album "Time"?
A) Can't Stop Me Now
B) It's Over
C) She Makes Me Happy
D) Time

Here are the answers to the last block of questions.

A71. Rod has now recorded five Great American Songbook Albums. They are Volume I: It Had To Be You; Volume II: As Time Goes By; Volume III: Stardust; Volume IV: Thanks For the Memory; Volume V: Fly Me To The Moon. "The Great American Songbook" is a series of albums by Rod that focuses on jazz standards and classic American songs.

A72. Rod collaborated with Cher for a cover version of "Bewitched, Bothered and Bewildered" which brings out Cher's deep soulful voice. In 2003 the song was released as a duet by Rod and Cher, as a single from Rod's second pop standards album, "As Time Goes By: the Great American Songbook, Volume II."

A73. Rod collaborated with Diana Ross for a cover version of "I've Got A Crush On You" which showcases Rod's stirring vocals in a song written by George Gershwin back in 1930. The Rod and Ross version is on the 2005 "Thanks for the Memory: the Great American Songbook, Volume IV" album.

A74. "Stardust: The Great American Songbook, Volume III" includes a duet with Dolly Parton on the song "Baby, It's Cold Outside."

A75. "It Had to Be You: The Great American Songbook" includes a version of "Blue Moon" featuring Eric Clapton.

A76. "You Wear It Well" is included in Rod's album "Never a Dull Moment" showcasing his knack for combining rock and folk elements.

A77. "Italian Girls", a song from on the "Never A Dull Moment" album reflects on the experiences of a young mod navigating through the lively and varied 1960s London scene.

A78. "Rhythm of My Heart" is one of the hits from the 1991 album "Vagabond Heart."

A79. "Purple Heather" is covered by Rod on the "Gasoline Alley" album, showcasing his affinity for traditional songs.

A80. "She Makes Me Happy" was the lead single from Rod's album "Time."

Let's have some lyrics related questions.

Q81. Which song starts with the lyrics, "May the good Lord be with you down every road you roam"?
A) Forever Young
B) Have I Told You Lately
C) Sailing
D) You're in My Heart

Q82. Which song starts with the lyrics, "Ever since I was a kid at school, I messed around with all the rules"?
A) Hot Legs
B) I Was Only Joking
C) Some Guys Have All The Luck
D) What's Made Milwaukee Famous

Q83. Which song contains the lyrics, "Spread your wings and let me come inside"?
A) Da Ya Think I'm Sexy?
B) Lost In You
C) Tonight's the Night (Gonna Be Alright)
D) You're in My Heart

Q84. Which song starts with the lyrics, "Early in the morning I can't sleep, I can't work, and I can't eat"?
D) Infatuation
B) This Old Heart of Mine
C) You Wear It Well
A) You're in My Heart

Q85. Which song starts with the line, "I didn't know what day it was when you walked into the room"?
A) Every Beat Of My Heart
B) Reason to Believe
C) You Wear It Well
D) You're in My Heart

Q86. Which song features the lyrics, "I wish that I knew what I know now, when I was younger"?
A) Faith Of The Heart
B) Lost In You
C) Ooh La La
D) Sweet Surrender

Q87. Which song starts with, "Stay away from my window, stay away from my back door too"?
A) Da Ya Think I'm Sexy?
B) Oh! No Not My Baby

C) Passion
D) Tonight's the Night

Q88. What song includes the lyrics, "Can you hear me, can you hear me through the dark night, far away"?
A) Maggie May
B) Sailing
C) Tonight I'm Yours
D) You Wear It Well

Q89. What song starts with the lyrics, "If I listened long enough to you, I'd find a way to believe that it's all true"?
A) My Heart Can't Tell You No
B) Passion
C) Reason To Believe
D) Young Turks

Q90. Which song starts with, "When my friends told me you had someone new, I didn't believe a single word was true"?
A) My Heart Can't Tell You No
B) Oh! No Not My Baby
C) Passion
D) Some Guys Have All The Luck

Here are the answers to the lyrics related questions.

A81. "Forever Young" starts with the lyrics "May the good Lord be with you down every road you roam." The song, with its heartfelt lyrics and melodious tune, is one of Rod's most enduring and beloved compositions, conveying a timeless message of love and well wishes.

A82. "I Was Only Joking" begins with the lyrics "Ever since I was a kid at school, I messed around with all the rules."

A83. The lyrics "Spread your wings and let me come inside" are from "Tonight's the Night (Gonna Be Alright)." This song, known for its suggestive and intimate lyrics, became a major hit, reflecting Rod's versatile musical style and his ability to convey emotion and sensuality through his music.

A84. "Infatuation" starts with the lyrics "Early in the morning I can't sleep, I can't work and I can't eat." This song, known for its catchy melody and relatable theme, highlights Rod's songwriting abilities and his knack for creating engaging and memorable music.

A85. "You're in My Heart" starts with the line "I didn't know what day it was when you walked into the room."

A86. The lyrics "I wish that I knew what I know now, when I was younger" are from "Ooh La La", depicting the theme of learned wisdom over time. The song is on the 1998 album "When We Were the New Boys". The song was originally recorded by Faces in 1973.

A87. "Tonight's the Night" starts with the lyrics "Stay away from my window, stay away from my back door too. Disconnect the telephone line, relax baby and draw that blind." This song, known for its suggestive lyrics and smooth melody, is one of Rod's iconic hits, reflecting the sensuality and passion often present in his music.

A88. "Sailing" contains the lyrics "Can you hear me, can you hear me through the dark night, far away. I am dying, forever trying to be with you, who can say."

A89. "Reason To Believe" starts with the lyrics "If I listened long enough to you I'd find a way to believe that it's all true. Knowing that you lied straight-faced while I cried. Still I look to find a reason to believe."

A90. "Oh! No Not My Baby" starts with the lyrics "When my friends told me you had someone new, I didn't believe a single word was true."

On to the next set of questions.

Q91. Which of these songs features the mandolin prominently?
A) Infatuation
B) Maggie May
C) Reason to Believe
D) What's Made Milwaukee Famous

Q92. Which album includes the hit single "Young Turks"?
A) Body Wishes
B) Camouflage
C) Every Beat of My Heart
D) Tonight I'm Yours

Q93. Which of Rod's songs was written as a tribute to his late friend, Danny Cordell?
A) Angel
B) I Don't Want To Talk About It
C) Mandolin Wind
D) The Killing of Georgie

Q94. Which album features the hit single "Forever Young"?
A) A Spanner in the Works
B) Every Beat of My Heart

C) Out of Order
D) Vagabond Heart

Q95. What genre does Rod's album "Another Country" primarily represent?
A) Country
B) Folk Rock
C) Pop
D) Rock

Q96. Which of Rod's albums was dedicated to his former girlfriend, Britt Ekland?
A) A Night on the Town
B) Atlantic Crossing
C) Blondes Have More Fun
D) Foot Loose & Fancy Free

Q97. Which of Rod's albums is subtitled 'A Rock Opera'?
A) An Old Raincoat Won't Ever Let You Down
B) Atlantic Crossing
C) Gasoline Alley
D) The Tears Of Hercules

Q98. Which song features a prominent harmonica played by Rod himself?
A) Gasoline Alley

B) Maggie May
C) Mandolin Wind
D) What's Made Milwaukee Famous

Q99. Which of Rod's albums was released in 1991 and includes a cover of Tom Waits' "Tom Traubert's Blues"?
A) A Spanner in the Works
B) Out of Order
C) Vagabond Heart
D) When We Were the New Boys

Q100. Which album, released in 2009, includes Rod's interpretations of classic soul songs?
A) Soulbook
B) Soul Boy
C) Soul Country
D) Soul Me A River

Here is the latest set of answers.

A91. "Maggie May" features the mandolin prominently. Played by Ray Jackson, the mandolin adds a distinctive and memorable sound to the song, contributing to its timeless appeal and its status as one of Rod's signature tunes.

A92. "Young Turks" is included on the "Tonight I'm Yours" album and became one of Rod's most popular songs.

A93. "Angel" was written by Rod as a tribute to his late friend, Danny Cordell, and is included in his album "Never a Dull Moment."

A94. "Forever Young" is included in Rod's album "Out of Order," and remains one of his enduring hits.

A95. "Another Country" primarily represents the folk-rock genre, showcasing his versatility as an artist.

A96. Rod's album "A Night on the Town" was dedicated to his former girlfriend, actress Britt Ekland.

A97. "An Old Raincoat Won't Ever Let You Down" is subtitled 'A Rock Opera,' highlighting its narrative and thematic elements.

A98.Rod plays the harmonica in "Gasoline Alley" showcasing his multifaceted musical talents.

A99. Rod's album "Vagabond Heart," released in 1991, features a cover of Tom Waits' "Tom Traubert's Blues."

A100. "Soulbook" features Rod's interpretations of classic soul songs, demonstrating his love for the genre and his ability to bring his unique vocal style to a diverse range of musical compositions.

Let's have some more questions.

Q101. Which album features the song "Reason to Believe"?
A) An Old Raincoat Won't Ever Let You Down
B) Every Picture Tells a Story
C) Gasoline Alley
D) Never a Dull Moment

Q102. What award did Rod receive at the Brit Awards in 1993?
A) British Album of the Year
B) British Male Solo Artist
C) British Single of the Year
D) Outstanding Contribution to Music

Q103. Which year did Rod release the album "Time"?
A) 2011
B) 2013
C) 2015
D) 2017

Q104.Which year did Rod perform at the FIFA World Cup concert in Rio de Janeiro, Brazil?
A) 2006
B) 2010

C) 2014
D) 2018

Q105. Which song was inspired by the Turkish invasion of Cyprus in 1974?
A) I Don't Want to Talk About It
B) Sailing
C) The First Cut Is the Deepest
D) Windswept

Q106. Which album features the hit single "Infatuation"?
A) Body Wishes
B) Camouflage
C) Every Beat of My Heart
D) Out of Order

Q107. Which album includes a cover of Van Morrison's song "Have I Told You Lately"?
A) A Spanner in the Works
B) Human
C) Vagabond Heart
D) When We Were the New Boys

Q108. Which album was dedicated to his parents?
A) A Spanner in the Works
B) Human

C) Vagabond Heart
D) When We Were the New Boys

Q109. Which album includes a cover of Sam Cooke's "Twistin' the Night Away"?
A) A Night on the Town
B) Atlantic Crossing
C) Never a Dull Moment
D) Smiler

Q110. What year was "Sailing" released?
A) 1975
B) 1977
C) 1979
D) 1981

Here is the latest set of answers.

A101. The album "An Old Raincoat Won't Ever Let You Down" features the song "Reason to Believe."

A102. Rod received the Outstanding Contribution to Music award at the Brit Awards in 1993, recognising his enduring influence on music.

A103. Rod released the album "Time" in 2013.

A104. Rod Stewart performed at the FIFA World Cup concert in Rio de Janeiro, Brazil in 2014, celebrating the global football event.

A105. "Sailing" although widely interpreted as a romantic or nautical song, was actually inspired by the Turkish invasion of Cyprus in 1974. The song's lyrics were penned by Gavin Sutherland with the effects of the conflict in mind, reflecting the depth and multifaceted nature of songwriting inspirations.

A106. The album "Camouflage" features the hit single "Infatuation."

A107. "Vagabond Heart" includes a cover of Van Morrison's "Have I Told You Lately." Rod's rendition of this song is widely acclaimed, highlighting his ability to interpret and convey the emotional depth of songs written by other artists.

A108. The album "Vagabond Heart" was dedicated by Rod to his parents.

A109. The album "Atlantic Crossing" includes a cover of Sam Cooke's song "Twistin' the Night Away."

A110. "Sailing" was released in 1975. It became a signature song of Rod and it achieved considerable chart success.

Here is the next set of questions.

Q111. What was Rod diagnosed with in 2000?
A) Laryngitis
B) Thyroid cancer
C) Vocal cord paralysis
D) Vocal nodules

Q112. What is the title of Rod's 2012 Christmas album?
A) Christmas With Rod
B) Merry Christmas, Baby
C) Rod's Christmas Classics
D) Rod Stewart's Christmas Special

Q113. Which album from the 2000s includes the hit "I Can't Deny It"?
A) Another Country
B) Human
C) Soulbook
D) When We Were The New Boys

Q114. Which guitarist and songwriter has Rod had a long-time collaboration with?
A) Jeff Beck
B) Jim Cregan
C) Martin Quittenton

D) Ronnie Wood

Q115. Which song does Rod Stewart sing about a lover who is leaving because she's going back to school?
A) Maggie May
B) Sailing
C) Tonight's the Night
D) You're in My Heart

Q116. Which of the following songs was written by Rod about the death of a friend due to a violent crime?
A) Blood Red Roses
B) I Don't Want To Talk About It
C) The Killing of Georgie
D) You're In My Heart

Q117. Which song did Rod write for his children?
A) Forever Young
B) Have I Told You Lately
C) The First Cut is the Deepest
D) You're in My Heart

Q118. Which of the following songs was originally recorded by the Sutherland Brothers before being covered by Rod?

A) I Don't Want to Talk About It
B) Maggie May
C) Sailing
D) You Wear It Well

Q119. Which album marked Rod's return to songwriting after a significant break?
A) Another Country
B) Blood Red Roses
C) The Tears of Hercules
D) Time

Q120. Which album features a duet with Helicopter Girl?
A) Another Country
B) Blood Red Roses
C) Human
D) Time

Here is the latest set of answers.

A111. In 2000, Rod was diagnosed with thyroid cancer, which affected his voice. After surgery, he had to re-learn singing due to the impact the cancer had on his vocal cords. However, he made a triumphant return to music and continues to inspire with his resilience and passion for singing.

A112. Rod's Christmas album from 2012 is titled "Merry Christmas, Baby." It features a collection of holiday classics and has received substantial acclaim for its festive atmosphere and Rod's distinctive vocal styling.

A113. "I Can't Deny It" is a hit from Rod's album "Human," released in 2001. This album marked a shift in his musical style and the song, in particular, received favorable reviews for its catchy melody and Stewart's distinctive vocals.

A114. Rod has had a long-time collaboration with guitarist and songwriter Jim Cregan. Cregan has co-written several songs with Rod and played guitar on numerous albums, contributing significantly to the sound and success of Stewart's music.

A115. In "Maggie May," Rod sings about a lover who plans on leaving him to go back to school. This song is a narrative of a doomed romantic entanglement with a woman who has other priorities, showcasing Stewart's ability to convey complex emotional scenarios through his music.

A116. "The Killing of Georgie" is a song written about the death of a friend due to a violent, hate-motivated crime. The song's narrative and emotional depth underscore Rod's songwriting abilities and his capacity to address serious and heartfelt themes through his music.

A117. "Forever Young" was written by Rod with his children in mind, particularly his son Sean and daughter Kimberly, who were eight and nine years old at the time. The song's heartfelt lyrics and emotive melody convey his wishes and hopes for his children, showcasing his ability to create music that is deeply personal yet universally relatable.

A118. "Sailing" was originally recorded by the Sutherland Brothers before being famously covered by Rod Stewart. Stewart's rendition of the song gave it a new lease of life and became one of his signature songs, demonstrating his ability to bring his unique style to existing pieces of music.

A119. "Time," released in 2013, marked Rod's return to songwriting after a significant break. This album, featuring original material penned by Rod, was received warmly by fans and critics alike, heralding a creative resurgence and reaffirming his status as a prolific songwriter.

A120. Rod's album "Human" released in 2001, features a duet with Helicopter Girl, highlighting Rod's willingness to collaborate with a diverse range of artists and explore different musical styles and sounds throughout his career.

Let's have some more lyrics related questions.

Q121. What song starts with the lyrics, "I would have given you all of my heart, but there's someone who's torn it apart"?
A) Maggie May
B) Sailing
C) The First Cut Is The Deepest
D) The Killing Of Georgie

Q122. What song starts with "I can tell by your eyes that you've probably been cryin' forever"?
A) Handbags And Gladrags
B) I Don't Want To Talk About It
C) My Heart Can't Tell You No
D) Reason To Believe

Q123. What song includes the lyrics, "Alone in a crowd on a bus after working, I'm dreaming. The guy next to me has a girl in his arms, my arms are empty"?
A) Every Beat Of My Heart
B) Some Guys Have All The Luck
C) You Wear It Well
D) Young Turks

Q124. What Faces song starts with the lyrics, "In the mornin' don't say you love me cause I'll only kick you out of the door"?
A) Cindy Incidentally
B) (I Know) I'm Losing You
C) Stay With Me
D) You Can Make Me Dance, Sing or Anything

Q125. What song starts with "Who's that knocking at my door, it's got to be a quarter to four"?
A) Baby Jane
B) Da Ya Think I'm Sexy?
C) Forever Young
D) Hot Legs

Q126. Which song starts with the lyrics, "In these days of changing ways, so called liberated days, a story comes to mind of a friend of mine"?
A) Angel
B) The Killing Of Georgie
C) Tonight I'm Yours
D) Young Turks

Q127. What song starts with the lyrics, "Ever see a blind man cross the road, trying to make the other side?"

A) Ain't Love A Bitch
B) Handbags And Gladrags
C) This Old Heart Of Mine
D) What's Made Milwaukee Famous

Q128. Which song contains the lyrics, "She sits alone waiting for suggestions"?
A) Baby Jane
B) Da Ya Think I'm Sexy?
C) Every Beat Of My Heart
D) Some Guys Have All The Luck

Q129. Which song includes the lyrics, "When I give my heart again, I know it's gonna last forever"?
A) Baby Jane
B) Handbags And Gladrags
C) Passion
D) Young Turks

Q130. What song starts with the lyrics, "She sits alone, waiting for suggestions, he's so nervous, avoiding all the questions"?
A) Da Ya Think I'm Sexy
B) This Old Heart Of Mine
C) Tonight I'm Yours
D) You Wear It Well

Here are the lyrics related answers.

A121. "The First Cut Is The Deepest" starts with the lyrics "I would have given you all of my heart but there's someone who's torn it apart and she's taken just all that I had, but if you want, I'll try to love again."

A122. "Reason To Believe" starts with the lyrics "I can tell by your eyes that you've probably been cryin' forever and the stars in the sky don't mean nothin' to you, they're a mirror."

A123. "Some Guys Have All The Luck" which was recorded in 1984 includes the lyrics "Alone in a crowd on a bus after working, I'm dreaming. The guy next to me has a girl in his arms, my arms are empty"

A124. "Stay With Me" recorded in 1971 by Faces with Rod as lead singer starts with the lyrics "In the mornin' don't say you love me cause I'll only kick you out of the door."

A125. "Hot Legs" begins with the lyrics "Who's that knocking at my door, it's got to be a quarter to four". Hot Legs was released in 1978 and is a blues-rocker with an incredible guitar riff.

A126 The Killing Of Georgie starts with the lyrics "In these days of changing ways so called liberated days a story comes to mind of a friend of mine." The themes covered in the song were groundbreaking when it was released in 1976.

A127. "Handbags And Gladrags" starts with the lyrics "Ever see a blind man cross the road trying to make the other side? Ever seen a young girl growing old trying to make herself a bride?"

A128. The lyrics "She sits alone waiting for suggestions" is from "Da Ya Think I'm Sexy?"

A129. The lyrics "When I give my heart again, I know it's gonna last forever" are from "Baby Jane."

A130. "Da Ya Think I'm Sexy?" starts with the lyrics "She sits alone, waiting for suggestions, he's so nervous, avoiding all the questions"?

OK, onto the next set of questions.

Q131. Which of these songs is based on a poem by Tim Hardin?
A) Handbags and Gladrags
B) I Was Only Joking
C) Mandolin Wind
D) Reason to Believe

Q132. Who does Rod duet with on the song "We Three Kings" on the album "Merry Christmas, Baby"?
A) Marsha Ambrosius
B) Mary J. Blige
C) Toni Braxton
D) Mariah Carey

Q133. Which film features "Faith of the Heart" as the theme song?
A) Patch Adams
B) Playing by Heart
C) The Magic of Marciano
D) Three to Tango

Q134. Which album includes the song "Love Touch"?
A) Camouflage

B) Every Beat of My Heart
C) Out of Order
D) Vagabond Heart

Q135. Which category was Rod inducted into the UK Music Hall of Fame in 2007?
A) Diamond Award
B) Gold Award
C) Icon Award
D) Legend Award

Q136. Rod's distinctive raspy voice is the result of a throat condition he developed after which event?
A) A concert in a smoky club
B) A football match
C) A thyroid operation
D) A vocal cord surgery

Q137. Which TV documentary series used "Sailing" as the theme tune?
A) Planet Earth
B) Sailor
C) The Blue Planet
D) The World at War

Q 138. Which album has a title that refers to an idiom meaning to live in luxury?
A) A Night on the Town
B) Blondes Have More Fun
C) Every Picture Tells a Story
D) Foot Loose & Fancy Free

Q139. What is Rod's largest ever concert audience?
A) over 1 million
B) over 2 million
C) over 3 million
D) over 4 million

Q140. Which of these songs was originally recorded by Tom Waits?
A) Downtown Train
B) Rhythm of My Heart
C) Some Guys Have All the Luck
D) Young Turks

Here is the lates set of answers.

A131. Tim Hardin was one of the great songwriters of the 1960s. Many of his songs were covered and made famous during his lifetime. "Reason to Believe" is based on a poem by Tim Hardin. The song, a reflection on disappointment and belief, showcases Rod's ability to translate poetic narratives into compelling musical compositions, highlighting the intersection of literature and music in his work.

A132. Rod duets with Mary J. Blige on the song "We Three Kings" on the "Merry Christmas, Baby" album.

A133. "Faith of the Heart" is a song written by Diane Warren and performed by Rod, for the soundtrack to the 1998 film 'Patch Adams', which starred Robin Williams.

A134. "Love Touch" is included in the 1986 album "Every Beat of My Heart." The song was prominently featured in the Robert Redford film 'Legal Eagles' and it embodies Rod's characteristic blend of rock and pop elements.

A135. In 2007, Rod was inducted into the UK Music Hall of Fame, receiving the Icon Award. This accolade honors his extraordinary career, spanning multiple decades, and celebrates his contributions to music and his status as one of the most recognizable and influential artists in the industry.

A136. Rod's distinctive raspy voice is attributed to a vocal cord surgery he underwent. The surgery altered the texture of his voice, giving it a distinctive gravelly quality that has become one of his defining characteristics and has contributed to his unique sound and style in the music industry.

A137. "Sailing" was used as the theme for the TV documentary series 'Sailor.' This series followed the life aboard the aircraft carrier HMS Ark Royal, and the song's emotive and poignant melody complemented the visual storytelling of the seafaring life and the challenges faced by the sailors.

A138. The title of the album "Foot Loose & Fancy Free" refers to an idiom meaning to live without any restrictions or obligations, often in luxury or leisure. This title reflects the album's energetic and liberating sound, showcasing Rod's dynamic musical range and his penchant for blending various musical styles.

A139. Rod performed in front of a reported 4.2 million fans at a spectacular New Year's Eve concert in 1994 at Copacabana Beach, Rio de Janeiro, Brazil. It is officially the largest concert of all time! It even earned a spot in the Guinness World Records.

A140. "Downtown Train" released in 1988 by Rod was originally recorded by Tom Waits. Rod's version of the song brought a new level of commercial success and mainstream appeal, showcasing his ability to reinterpret songs and make them his own, while maintaining the essence of the original composition.

Here goes with the final set of questions.

Q141. What musical genre primarily influences the album "A Spanner in the Works"?
B) Blues
B) Folk
C) Jazz
D) Pop

Q142. Which magazine named Rod Stewart Rock Star of the Year' in 1978?
A) Billboard
B) Melody Maker
C) NME
D) Rolling Stone

Q143. Which song does Rod reference being "in the scullery soaking to the skin"?
A) Maggie May
B) Sailing
C) The Killing of Georgie
D) Young Turks

Q144. What is Rod's best selling single?
A) Maggie May
B) Sailing
C) The Killing of Georgie

D) Young Turks

Q145. Which song is considered a follow up to "Maggie May"?
A) Ain't Love A Bitch
B) I Was Only Joking
C) Tonight's the Night
D) You're in My Heart

Q146. Which of these can be seen as a signature look for Rod?
A) Flannel shirts
B) Hawaiian shirts
C) Leopard print outfits
D) Tuxedos

Q147. Which band recorded "In A Broken Dream" with Rod as lead vocalist?
A) Cobra Wee Lincoln
B) Copperhead Mee Hamilton
C) Mamba Dee Grant
D) Python Lee Jackson

Q148. How many Grammy Awards has Rod won?
A) 1
B) 11
C) 21

D) 31

Q149. What is the title of Rod Stewart's autobiography?
A) Every Picture Tells a Story: My Life
B) Forever Young: My Life in Music
C) Rod: The Autobiography
D) The Rod Stewart Story

Q150. When was Rod knighted?
A) 2012
B) 2014
C) 2016
D) 2018

Here is the final set of answers.

A141. "A Spanner in the Works," released in 1995, is primarily influenced by pop music. The album features a modern sound, blending various musical elements and demonstrating Stewart's adaptability and willingness to experiment with different genres and musical styles.

A142. In 1978, Rolling Stone magazine named Rod Stewart 'Rock Star of the Year,' a testament to his significant impact on the music scene during that time. This recognition highlighted his popularity, musical achievements, and influence in the rock music genre.

A143. In "Maggie May" Rod references being "in the scullery soaking to the skin." The line is part of the vivid narrative within the song, showcasing Rod's ability to paint detailed and immersive pictures through his lyrics, enhancing the storytelling element of his music.

A144. "Sailing" is Rod's best-selling song ever.

A145. "Ain't Love A Bitch" is widely recognised as the sequel to "Maggie May." The song's lyrics include, "Oh I didn't realise she made a first class fool out of me, Oh Maggie if you're still out there the rest is history." "Ain't Love a Bitch" was written by Rod Stewart and Gary Grainger for the 1978 album "Blondes Have More Fun". It was released as a single in 1979.

A146. Rod is known for his distinctive fashion taste, and yet he is regularly associated with leopard print outfits.

A147. Python Lee Jackson recorded "In A Broken Dream" in 1969 with Rod as lead vocalist. Rod was brought into the studio as a session musician to sing three tracks, and he was paid a set of car seat covers for his recording session. If you've never heard of the song before, it is worth tracking down on YouTube.

A148. Incredibly, Rod has won only one Grammy award. He won the Grammy award for Best Traditional Pop Vocal Album in 2005 for the album "Stardust...The Great American Songbook Volume III." Winning this prestigious award was a testament to Stewart's musical impact and his ability to bring fresh interpretations to classic

American songs, connecting them with new audiences.

A149. Rod's autobiography, published in 2012, is aptly titled 'Rod: The Autobiography.' It provides an intimate look into his life, career, and the music industry, offering fans insights into the man behind the iconic voice and timeless hits.

A150. Rod Stewart was knighted by Queen Elizabeth II in 2016 for his services to music and charity, acknowledging his substantial contributions over the years. This esteemed recognition underscores his significant contributions to the music industry, his extensive philanthropic efforts, and his enduring influence on the cultural landscape.

That's a great question to finish with.

That's it. I hope you enjoyed this book, and I hope you got most of the answers right. I also hope you learnt some new things about Sir Rod!

If you have any comments or if you saw anything wrong, please email rod@glowwormpress.com and we'll get the book updated.

Thanks for reading, and if you did enjoy the book, please leave a positive review on Amazon.

Printed in Great Britain
by Amazon

42849019R00050